WISE UP

The Savvy Consumer's Guide to Buying Insurance

HOME, RENTAL, AUTO & UMBRELLA EDITION

Amy R. Bach and John P. Sullivan

United
Policyholders™

Acknowledgments

United Policyholders dedicates this guide to investigative journalists and business reporters everywhere. Your work provides essential protection to consumers. Long may you thrive.

UP thanks and acknowledges the following contributors to this guide: Emily Rogan, Professor Brenda Cude, Ph.D., professional insurance agents David Shaffer, Shirley Brown, Larry Tencer, Joseph Vaccaro, Richie Clements and Corrin Trowbridge, wildfire survivor Susan Piper and Certified Financial Planners Larry Ginsburg and David Lawrence. Special thanks to Deeia Beck; Office of Public Insurance Counsel, J. Robert Hunter and the Consumer Federation of America, and the National Association of Insurance Commissioners' Transparency and Readability Working Group members and staff; Angie Nelson, Joel Laucher, Sara Robben.

Table of Contents

1 Introduction

2 Home Insurance

3   Renters Insurance

4   Auto Insurance

5 Umbrella Insurance

6 Filing an Insurance Claim

A Appendix: Worksheets

Introduction

Buying insurance isn't on anyone's top ten list of favorite ways to spend money. It's not a purchase you can enjoy driving, listening to or eating. But the fact is it's a necessity in our modern world. So congratulations on being a savvy consumer and taking advantage of this guide. This inside scoop on getting your money's worth when buying insurance comes from a non-profit organization called United Policyholders ("UP").

So whether you're buying it because you legally have to, or because you want to protect yourself and your assets, this guide is designed to help you buy policies that will pay when you need them to pay. A talking animal in an insurance commercial may be cute and funny, but he's not giving you what you need: the lowdown on buying real protection at a fair price. That's where UP's expertise comes in handy.

Since 1991 UP has been guiding and advocating for consumers in the world of insurance: Car crashes; disasters; lawsuits; claim and blame games; customer satisfaction; customer frustration; good faith; bad faith. Insurance companies that deliver; insurance companies that don't.

To keep our independence and credibility, we don't sell insurance and we don't accept funding from insurance companies. Never have. Never will.

If you're an insurance consumer—a "policyholder"—this book is for *you*. UP is *on your side*.

From the Oakland/Berkeley firestorm to Hurricane Katrina, Superstorm Sandy and after thousands of fires, floods, accidents and losses, UP has seen how insurance can fuel recovery. But we've also seen how insurers' profit motives can override the interests of their customers. Insurance is BIG business.

Use this guide to see through clever commercials that raise your expectations of protection, but mask the fine print that can cost you dearly when you file a claim. Use it to avoid wasting money and the painful and expensive "surprises" that can come when a policy you thought would be your safety net turns out to have gaping holes.

Most people never know their insurance is out of whack until after something bad happens and it's too late to fix it. If suddenly losing your home and possessions in a disaster isn't bad enough, imagine the shock of finding out that the insurance you have been paying for is far from enough to rebuild your home and replace its contents.

> AFTER A 2007 WILDFIRE IN SAN DIEGO COUNTY, a United Policyholders survey found that two-thirds of victims were underinsured by an average of more than $100,000.

We'll give you questions to ask when you buy and renew your policies from year to year, and guidance on the features that matter. Your insurance policies and the benefits they provide should be your personal financial safety net. Let's make them work for you ...

Keep in mind that each of the fifty states has its own laws and regulations and each insurance company has its own policy language and claim-handling guidelines.

For more information please visit us at:
www.uphelp.org and www.facebook.com/uphelp

Insurance lingo: Key words

Reviewing the terms below before you start will help you get the most out of this guide.

Actual Cash Value—The amount a willing buyer would have paid a willing seller for an item immediately before it was damaged or destroyed. Also sometimes called "Fair Market" or "Depreciated" value.

Additional Living Expense—One of the main categories of coverage in a home or renters policy. Sometimes labeled as "Temporary Living Expenses" or "Loss of Use." Covers additional rent, furniture rental, laundry, extra gas and other expenses you incur because you can't live in your home.

Bodily Injury Protection—One of the main categories of coverage in an auto policy. Covers medical and related expenses due to an injury accident.

Cancellation—An insurer or insured cancels a policy in the middle of the policy year or term. Non-payment or changes of ownership are the most common reasons for cancellations.

CLUE—("Comprehensive Loss and Underwriting Exchange")—An insurance loss/claim history database that insurers use to choose customers and set prices. Pay the small fee and get a copy of your CLUE report to see what insurers can see about you.

Collision/Comprehensive—Two categories in an auto policy that cover physical damage to your vehicle.

Declarations ("Dec") Page —Usually the cover or first page of a policy. Lists the names of the people, location, vehicle or items insured, the basic and extra coverages, limits and deductibles, and whether a lender or other entity is an additional insured on the policy.

Deductible—An amount the insurer will deduct from its payment on a loss. A deductible can be a flat dollar amount (e.g. $500) or a percentage (e.g. 2% of the insured value of the dwelling). You will not collect insurance benefits on a loss that falls below your deductible. The higher your deductible, the cheaper the policy should be and vice versa.

Let's say you choose a $1,000 deductible for your home insurance. A pipe bursts and causes $3,000 in damage. If your policy covers the loss, the insurance company deducts the $1,000 and owes you $2,000 toward the repairs.

TOTAL DAMAGE:	$3,000
YOUR DEDUCTIBLE:	$1,000
TOTAL YOU COLLECT:	**$2,000**

If the damage is only $800, you recover no benefits because the amount of loss is below the deductible.

Depreciation—Loss in value due to use and age.

Difference in Conditions ("DIC")—A policy that fills coverage gaps. Sometimes called a "wrap" or "wraparound" policy or rider.

Dwelling—A residence or home.

Endorsement—An add-on or change attached to your basic policy contract that either takes away or adds coverage or otherwise changes the contract. Also referred to as a "rider" or a "floater."

Exclusions and Limitations—The fine print legalese in insurance policies that limits the circumstances where the insurer will pay a claim and the timing and amounts of their payments.

Floater—*See* "Endorsement."

Indemnify—Agree to be financially responsible for losses or damage. An insurance policy is an indemnification contract. The insurance company agrees to indemnify you (make you whole in the event of a loss).

Insured—The person or persons covered by an insurance policy.

Insurer—A company that has agreed to take on risk in exchange for payment of a premium.

Inflation Adjustment Factor—A formula built in to most policies that adjusts policy limits upward to account for inflation. May or may not be enough to keep up with current prices of items, materials and labor.

Liability Coverage—Protects you if someone claims or sues, saying you are responsible for injury or damage to people or property. Liability coverage can cover legal fees plus the amount you are found responsible (or "liable") to pay.

Limits—The most you can collect under each coverage category in a policy. Inflation formulas and endorsements that change the basic policy can change the limits. Most policies have several different categories of coverage, each with its own limit.

Loss of Use—*See* "Additional Living Expense."

Non-Renewal—A notice you get when your insurer decides not to renew your policy when it expires.

Personal Excess Liability Coverage—*See* "Umbrella Coverage."

Policy—A contract specifying the amounts, limits and conditions of insurance coverage.

Policyholder—A person named in an insurance policy as the insured.

Premiums—Payments made to an insurance company to keep a policy in force. Premiums can be paid up front, monthly, annually or over the life of the policy.

Rate—The unit price an insurance company charges for a specific risk.

Replacement Value—The cost to repair or replace your home or stuff without a deduction for depreciation.

Rescission—A legal strategy an insurer can use to deny a claim and revoke a policy where the insured has made a misrepresentation on an application for coverage.

Rider—Added or subtracted coverage or conditions. *See* "Endorsement."

Risk Exposure—The possibility of loss or damage associated with a person, event or property. Insurance pricing is generally based on risk exposure (such as loss history, location, age, and for auto insurance, type of vehicle and driving record).

Surcharge—A price increase added to a basic insurance rate because of a specific condition or change in condition associated with the insured risk. Example: A speeding ticket can result in a surcharge on your auto insurance.

Umbrella Coverage—An insurance policy you buy if you have sizable assets to protect. This coverage adds to your home or auto policy by giving you higher limits and, in some cases, broader coverage. Umbrella coverage is usually reasonably priced and provides additional coverage for large lawsuits and serious accidents. Also known as "Personal Excess Liability" coverage.

Underinsured/Uninsured Motorist Coverage (UM/UIM)—Protection for losses caused by a driver with inadequate or no insurance.

How to shop for insurance

You can shop for insurance in a few minutes, or a few hours. You can use a professional agent or broker, you can call an insurer directly or you can use the Internet.

Fast and easy and on your own is usually okay for insuring a car. But if you want to properly insure a home and valuables, doing it on your own is risky. An experienced, consumer-oriented professional agent or broker who knows the marketplace can help you find superior coverage at a price you can afford. A knowledgeable agent will be up to speed on options. A helpful agent will take the time to understand your situation and guide you through your choices. A lazy or greedy agent will sell you too little or too much insurance.

Insurance companies are great at coming up with catchy, funny ads that convey warm and fuzzy feelings. But these ads paint a rosy picture of happiness and security that bears little connection to the reality of what insurance is, and what can happen when you need to use it. An insurance policy isn't a magic wand. It's a complicated legal contract sold to you by a company that's in business to make a profit.

SHOPPING TOOLS WE LIKE:

A Texas tool: Easy to use, points out what matters, such as coverage and limits for water damage:

www.uphelp.org/OPICtool

A California tool: Useful for comparing two or more policies:

www.uphelp.org/CAtool

These tools are helpful even If you don't live in one of these states.

When you need to use your insurance, fine print really matters. So take the time to shop. And not just for the cheapest price.

It's not easy to compare insurance policies, but thanks to the efforts of UP and other consumer advocates, this is changing. There are now free tools that let you do a side-by-side comparison between policies sold by different companies to see—for example—whether they include or exclude mold or sewer backup damage. In a growing number of states insurers are now required to post sample copies of their policies online. But even with these advances, working with a knowledgeable and helpful insurance agent will help you make the right decisions. "Off-the-shelf" home and renters insurance policies rarely cover all of your specific risks.

Professional insurance salespeople

A professional insurance salesperson is called an agent, broker or adviser. Agents and brokers are regulated by the government, and in most states, must pass a licensing exam and continuing education requirements. Their job is to help you understand your insurance needs and options and submit an application to one or more insurance companies. As in any profession, some are better than others.

Agents are compensated by commissions that are a percentage of your insurance premiums. Commission amounts vary by insurance company, and they can influence an agent's recommendations. An agent may steer you to the insurance company or policy that pays them a high commission. But it's very hard to know if they are doing that, so your best bet is to find an experienced agent with a good reputation, and keep good notes when you speak with them. One place to start is www.yapaquote.org.

Captive vs. Independent agents

"Captive Agents" work for one insurance company and can only place you with that company. Sometimes an agent's status is obvious (e.g. you see only one insurance company logo displayed in their office) and sometimes it's not.

"Independent Agents" are sometimes referred to as "brokers" because they can insure you with one of several insurance companies. Careful consumers often prefer to use independent agents because they can gather competitive quotes for you to compare and they can recommend the best combination of price, coverage and deductible. Some independent agents can handle all your insurance needs: home, auto, disability, medical, umbrella and life insurance policies. The more complex your situation is and the more assets you need to protect, the more helpful it is to work with an independent agent familiar with several different policies.

A person selling you insurance in any state has a legal duty to be honest. What differs from state to state is whether or not that person has a legal duty to take care of *your* specific insurance needs, and whether you can hold them accountable if they fail to do so.

If your insurance needs are basic, get quotes from captive *and* independent agents. You may find that the lowest cost coverage is through a captive agent. But if you follow this strategy, pay extra attention to policy limits and exclusions and ask plenty of questions to avoid being underinsured.

Since the terms "broker" and "independent agent" can be confusing, the important thing is to ask the person you are dealing with:

1) Who do you work for?
2) How many insurance companies do you represent?
3) How are you compensated?
4) What insurance company and policy do you recommend for me and why?

You may feel uncomfortable asking an insurance salesperson about how much their commission will be and whether they have a bonus incentive to steer you to one insurer over another, but you should. Their answers to the above 4 questions will help you figure out whether you can rely on them to point you in the best direction.

"Bundling" your policies

Insurers and agents that sell car, home and umbrella policies will usually steer you to buy all your policies through one insurance company. Most tell you you'll get a discount for "bundling." But each insurer has their own rules for pricing ("rating") customers, handling claims and raising (or not raising) your rates after you file a claim. Before you insure your home and car with the same company, ask about those rules. Get a few quotes just for auto and just for home to make sure you'll actually be paying less if you package them. Also, some insurers are more experienced in insuring homes than cars and vice versa. You may find a better quality and priced policy for your home and for your car from two different companies. **Bundling can be a good deal but it's not automatically or always the way to go. Ask questions, get quotes and compare.**

Picking an insurance company

Insurance companies are not all the same and the quality of their products vary. The most important factors to consider are:

POLICY LIMITS AND EXCLUSIONS—Some insurance companies offer better coverage and fewer exclusions at a higher price. Others offer lower premiums for coverage that is less comprehensive. Focus on adequately insuring the "big ticket" items (your home's structure, basement, roof and foundation, your car and your personal liability), and avoid policies that exclude water damage, mold, and cosmetic damage. Your objective is to create an economic safety net that meets your needs, priorities and budget.

PRICING—Comparing policies by price alone gives you only part of the info you need to make a good choice and put an economic safety net in place. You need to compare *quality* of coverage, not just price.

CLAIM RULES: POST CLAIM RATE INCREASES AND NON-RENEWAL RULES—Each insurer has guidelines that should tell you what will happen to your policy after you file a claim. Will one claim trigger a rate increase or non-renewal? Does fault and claim severity matter? Find out *before* you pick the insurer you'll be entrusting with your financial security.

REPUTATION—Insurance companies vary in what they cover and exclude, and how fairly and quickly they handle claims.

Here are a few ways to check out an insurance company's reputation and the quality of their policies:

- Ask a good independent agent who sells for a variety of insurers.
- Visit the website for the government agency in your state that oversees insurance companies. Most of them publish statistics on consumer complaints against each insurer. The State-by-State help section of www.uphelp.org has a link to the insurance regulatory agency in every state. Some offer comparison-shopping tools.
- Check out UP's post-disaster Roadmap to Recovery™ surveys at www.uphelp.org/surveyresults and see what people say about how their insurer handled their large or total loss claim.
- The Internet: You'll find useful information on websites that relate to insurance. Just be aware that most of them are aimed at selling you insurance. Websites that are not hosted by insurance companies such as www.uphelp.org, www.ConsumerReports.org and www.ValChoice.com are especially helpful when shopping for insurance.

- Word of mouth—Friends, neighbors and co-workers who've had personal experience with a claim can be helpful.

FINANCIAL STRENGTH—You want a financially strong insurance company that will be there and solvent if you need them to pay a claim. Insurance companies are rated by independent agencies like A.M. Best. You can research a company's financial rating at www.ambest.com.

"SURPLUS LINES" / "NON-ADMITTED" INSURERS—There are insurance companies that for business reasons have chosen not to fully comply with state licensing and regulation requirements. They operate lawfully, but are not covered by the "guaranty" funds that protect policyholders whose insurers go bankrupt. If your only option for buying insurance is through a non-admitted company (for example in high-risk flood areas), check their financial ratings to make sure they're strong. Although surplus insurers must comply with state and federal laws, government officials say they are harder to police than admitted insurers, and their policies tend to cost more than standard market policies.

"LPI" (LENDER PLACED) INSURANCE—Also known as "forced place," this is a type of insurance a bank or mortgage company buys for you and the cost gets added to your loan balance. Typically over-priced and low value, an LPI policy should be a last resort. Only buy an LPI policy if you have no other option.

POOLS, PLANS, PUBLIC/PRIVATE HYBRIDS—For some risks and in some areas, affordable insurance is not available. To fill the gaps, the state or federal government has stepped in to help by setting up hybrid public/private insurance companies. Examples include: Citizens Insurance in Florida and Louisiana, the Texas Windstorm Insurance Association, the California Earthquake Authority and the National Flood Insurance Program. If you live in a wildfire prone area and can't find home insurance, your state may offer a last resort option like the California "FAIR" plan (Fair Access to

Insurance Requirements). If your driving record is bad, your state may offer an auto policy through an "assigned risk" pool-type plan. If your only option is to buy insurance through one of these, we recommend the following:

- Ask about the limits, exclusions and gaps in coverage that are common with these programs so you know in advance what won't be covered. Many offer only "Actual Cash Value," not replacement value coverage.
- Try to keep a rainy day fund to cover insurance gaps. If your state offers tax incentives for a "Catastrophe Savings Account" look into setting one up.
- Continue to check for new options that may become available over time.

> ### Dropped by your insurance company?
> ### Don't panic, start shopping

Insurance policies are usually one-year contracts. When the year is up, three things can happen:

1) The insurer renews the policy by sending you a new contract with the same coverage and pricing as the old one.

2) The insurer sends a new policy with different coverage and pricing.

3) The insurer non-renews the policy. Most people refer to that third situation as being "dropped." Technically it's a "non-renewal."

If you get a non-renewal notice, you can contact the insurer to request reconsideration. If the insurer gave you the legally required advance notice and just doesn't want you as a customer any more, start shopping right away for a replacement policy and avoid panicking. Shop around, find the best option, lock in a policy then continue to check in from time to time on new options. Home and car insurance markets are dynamic, and new options become available over time.

Switching to a new insurer can have advantages: By comparison shopping, using the Internet and getting help, you may end up with better coverage at the same or even a better price.

If you have trouble finding replacement policy options and need shopping help, contact an experienced and reputable independent agent that can place you with a range of insurers. If you feel you've been non-renewed or cancelled unfairly, contact your State Department of Insurance. They can help you get information, file a complaint or offer guidance on a replacement policy. Some states have Market Assistance programs to help people find coverage in regions or for types of risks insurers are avoiding.

Home Insurance

What is home insurance?

Home insurance (also referred to as homeowners insurance) provides economic protection for a dwelling and its contents, in the event of a fire, theft, or disaster, with various exclusions and limitations. Flood, earth movement and earthquake damage are commonly excluded and must be insured separately. *Coverage for mold, water, sewer backup and pollution damage is often limited or excluded.* Most home policies cover loss of use (also called "Additional" or "Temporary" Living Expense) for alternate living arrangements while a home is being repaired or rebuilt. Most cover other structures, (detached garages, outbuildings, etc.), trees/shrubs/landscaping, and debris removal.

Home policies also provide liability coverage for accidents that occur at the property or are caused by the homeowner (or a family member or pet) away from the property. Liability coverage is for injuries, medical bills, damage to other people's property and defending you in a lawsuit.

Why buy home insurance?

If your home is damaged or destroyed by a fire or other calamity or you are the victim of a break in, home insurance provides money to repair or rebuild, replace necessities and possessions and cover temporary living expenses while the home is uninhabitable. If you have a mortgage, your lender will require you to buy basic insurance for at least the amount of your loan.

Insurance is the fastest and best source of money to repair or rebuild after a loss. It is a myth that the government will bail you out after a disaster. Grants are sometimes available from FEMA after a disaster, but the *average* amount is under $5,000. Charitable aid almost never covers the cost of rebuilding a home, and loans need to be paid back. Getting a government grant or charitable aid can take years.

A DAY IN
The (Real) Life

A girl threw a Frisbee to her dog on a sunny day in the park. The dog ran across a bike path to catch it, causing a cyclist to fall and break her wrist. The cyclist, who earned her living as a writer, sued the girl's family for medical costs, lost wages and pain and suffering. The girl's family's home insurance ultimately paid several hundred thousand dollars to settle the case, protecting the family from a significant financial loss.

Home insurance policies also protect your assets if you are hit with a claim or lawsuit related to an accidental non-vehicle injury on or off the premises of your home.

Coverage categories

A home policy should contain the important categories or "buckets" of protection. Most have a maximum benefit limit, deductible and exclusions. Some policies provide one combined single limit for all categories of coverage.

COVERAGE A—Dwelling (the house itself).

COVERAGE B—Other Structures (detached garages, sheds, retaining walls, etc.).

COVERAGE C—Personal Property (furniture, clothing and other possessions, also referred to as "Contents").

COVERAGE D—Loss of Use (costs you incur as a result of a covered loss because you can't live in your home during repairs/rebuilding), also called Additional Living Expenses or "ALE."

COVERAGE E—Personal Liability (protection against claims someone makes against you for accidents and losses, on or off the insured property).

COVERAGE F—Medical payments to others (covers medical bills if someone is injured on your property, regardless of fault, or off the property if caused by a family member or pet).

ADDITIONAL COVERAGES—Can include building code upgrades, (ordinance/law compliance), debris removal, sewer and drain backup, ID theft/fraud, lock replacement, green rebuilding upgrades, loss assessment fees and fire department charges, "scheduled" personal property (jewelry, electronics, fine art, silver, antiques and collectibles, etc.) and home-based business property and operations.

Deductibles

Deductibles are an amount your insurance company will deduct from its payment to you on a loss. Almost every policy has a deductible. You may suffer a loss and collect no insurance benefits if the amount of the loss is less than the deductible. The good thing about deductibles is that you can raise them to reduce the cost of your insurance.

NOTE: You'll pay higher premiums for a policy with a lower deductible. Because claims are relatively rare, for most people, choosing a high deductible is a good money-saving option.

When shopping for insurance, especially earthquake or hurricane coverage, deductible options are a big decision point. Traditionally deductibles were flat dollar amounts; $250, $500, etc., but percentage deductibles from 1% to as high as 15% have become the norm for earthquake, windstorm, hurricane, hail and even some home policies.

UP recommends that you pick the highest deductible you feel comfortable with, then pay for small damage and claims out of pocket. Why?

1) Every insurance claim you file can put you in a higher risk category and cause you to pay more over the long term for your policies. (See "Get a Clue," page 30)

2) You don't have to *pay* the amount of your deductible toward repairs before your insurer will pay benefits. You just recover less in benefits.

But a high deductible is a trade-off: If your deductible is $2,500 and your toilet overflows and ruins a wood floor, causing $2,200 in damage, you won't see an insurance payment. That loss was below your deductible. A $1,000 deductible on a home policy is a reasonable choice for most people.

Toilet overflows, damages bathroom floor and ceiling below.
Repairs will cost $2.500
A policy with a $1,000 deductible will cover $1,500 of the repairs (unless it excludes water damage) while a policy with a $500 deductible will cover $2,000 of the repairs.

Some insurance policies have more than one deductible; one for dwelling damage and another for contents, or one applicable to a theft or fire claim and another for a windstorm/hurricane claim. Do your best to understand the different deductibles in your policy.

High winds pull off a section of your roof, causing rain to soak a part of your attic.
Repairs will cost $13,000. Insured value of the house is $200,000.

A policy with a 5% wind deductible will pay $3,000 of the repairs (the deductible is 5% of $200,000).

Things to consider when buying home insurance

1 A HOME IS A MAJOR ASSET. 15 MINUTES ISN'T ENOUGH TIME TO PROPERLY INSURE IT—These days you can buy insurance for your home in less than fifteen minutes, but UP strongly recommends against that. Spend time making sure you buy enough and the right kind. And as tempting as it is to buy the cheapest policy you can find, we recommend against that too, because the cheapest policies usually result in underinsurance. Experts estimate that two thirds of American homes are underinsured.

The old saying, "Don't be penny wise and pound-foolish" applies here. Comparison shop on price and quality: Get price quotes, in writing, from at least three sources and make sure you're comparing "apples to apples" in terms of what's covered and what's excluded. Don't accept price quotes over the phone. Ask for a detailed written quote and description of coverage by email, U.S. mail or fax.

2 **DON'T BLINDLY TRUST THAT YOUR INSURANCE COMPANY HAS YOU FULLY COVERED**—In many cases, agents will gather basic info from you about your home's age and size and give you a fast price quote. Their main objective is to sign you up as a paying customer. Insurance salespeople usually try to win your business on low price and not quality or adequacy of coverage. They will assure you you're fully covered but you may not be.

The software that most insurers, agents and shopping websites use when giving you a quote for a home insurance policy is based on generic/tract homes and national average construction pricing. It spits out a quote quickly to make the sale. Quick home insurance quotes rarely insure a home to value. They leave out unique features, custom construction, local conditions and building codes. Most agents and insurers would rather close a sale than quote you the real price for full insurance.

3 **TRUST BUT VERIFY, DOUBLE CHECK POLICY LIMITS**—As a *homeowner* your key objective should be to "insure to value." The dollar amount of your Dwelling or Structure limit should be as close as possible to what it would cost to rebuild your home if it burned to the ground and had to be completely rebuilt. Your coverage for other items, (Contents, Loss of Use, Landscaping, Debris Removal etc.) will most likely be set by the insurer as a percentage of the "A" amount, so it is important to get the right value for Coverage A.

Here are some of the ways you can double check the adequacy of your home insurance:

- **The Agent Method**—Ask your insurance agent to run replacement cost estimates on your home and provide you with the calculations.

- **The Professional Appraisal**—Arrange for a professional home replacement cost estimator or building contractor to come to your house and provide an estimate of the cost to rebuild. Some insurers offer this service at no charge.

- **The E2 Value Method**—Visit www.e2Value.com and spend a half-hour or so answering questions about your home in this online home replacement cost-estimating software.

- **The Rough Math Method**—Multiply your home's square footage of living space by the going rate for construction costs for a home of its type in your city or town.

4 BE CLEAR ABOUT YOUR INSURANCE GOALS AND KEEP GOOD NOTES—In most cases when you buy insurance, the insurer or agent sets the policy limits, and you don't question or second-guess them. But guess what? If you have a loss and it turns out those limits were too low for what you need to repair or rebuild, you'll be in a tough spot.

In most states, you—the policyholder who relied on the insurer or agent's expertise to set the limits— will be left to cover the gap.

When it comes to legal responsibility for setting the limits in your policy— *U.S. laws don't reflect reality.* Unless you have proof that an agent or insurer

> **INSURE TO VALUE:** If you want to protect the financial investment you've made in your home, you need to spend time insuring it to value. Short cuts will result in a home that's not properly insured. You don't want to waste money over-insuring you home, but you don't want to underinsure it.

specifically promised you that the limits would be adequate to replace your home, the underinsurance gap is your problem, not theirs. If a dispute arises over your insurance shortfall, in the words of TV reporter Nancy Grace after Hurricane Katrina: "He with the most notes wins."

5 **AIM FOR REPLACEMENT VALUE NOT REAL ESTATE VALUE**—Insure your home for the amount it would cost to rebuild, not its sale/ real estate value. These are two very different things. You'll need to know your home's size (how many square feet of living space) and get a general idea of local building costs (per square foot) for a home of similar quality and materials.

6 **FINE PRINT AND EXTRAS THAT MATTER**—Your best bet is to buy an "All-Risk" policy that provides broad coverage, not a "Named Perils" policy. A broad form policy covers a wide range of risks except those specifically excluded. A "Named Perils" policy only covers those risks that are specifically listed.

Basic insurance covers "as was" and won't pay for improvements/upgrades required by local or state building codes. After a loss, older foundations, electrical and plumbing systems and roofs often need to be upgraded to current codes for building permit approval and the costs can be very substantial. You won't be able to legally repair or rebuild your home unless your project is in compliance with the current building codes in your area. So especially if you have an older home, make sure to buy "code upgrade" coverage.

EXTRAS THAT MATTER:

• Building code compliance

• Extended replacement cost

• Drain and sewer backup

Ask about the cost of adding Extended Replacement Cost ("ERC") coverage (or even the rare "Guaranteed Replacement Cost," if available). Buy the most ERC protection you can afford—it is usually sold as an extra 25-100% of coverage above your "Coverage A" Dwelling limit. ERC coverage is generally a bargain well worth the price. It gives you a cushion in case your policy limit isn't enough to cover higher construction costs that often occur after natural disasters.

7   TAILOR YOUR PERSONAL PROPERTY COVERAGE—In most policies, Coverage "C" is for your "stuff" (contents/personal property). If possible, insure your stuff for Replacement Cost Value ("RCV")—not Actual Cash Value ("ACV") (i.e. depreciated or "used" value). Replacement Cost Value coverage costs more but is usually well worth paying for.

When you buy a home policy, some insurers will ask how much contents insurance you want and give you options. Others will automatically set your contents coverage as a percentage of your dwelling coverage. It is common for an insurer to set your contents coverage at 70% of your dwelling coverage. That may be the right amount or it may be more than you need.

TYPICAL SUB-LIMITS AND CAPS*:

$ 200 limit on money, banknotes, coins

$1,000 on securities, accounts, deeds, stamps

$1,000 on jewelry, watches, fur

$2,500 on silverware

$1,000 on trailers

$2,000 on firearms

$2,500 on business personal property

*Dollar amounts and limited items may be different with each insurance company.

If you work from home and/or have valuables such as jewelry, art, antiques, rugs, collectibles, firearms, musical instruments, or electronics, you may need to adjust your coverage. Most policies have sub-limits and caps for specific items. To fully insure high value items, you may need extra or "scheduled" coverage. Fine art and jewelry should be professionally appraised.

8 KNOW YOUR LOCAL RISKS AND COVER THEM—Are you in an area at risk for floods, landslides, hurricanes or earthquakes?

If you're not sure, enter your zip code at www.DisasterSafety.org. To find out if you're in a flood zone, go to www.floodsmart.gov. To find out if you are in high-risk area for earthquakes go to www. earthquake.usgs.gov/hazards.

Damage from floods, landslides and earthquakes are almost always *excluded* in standard policies. If you want to be insured for those risks, you need to buy a policy or endorsement that specifically covers them. Other risks, such as damage from leaking pipes, roof leaks, or mold may or may not be covered. Ask your agent or insurer to explain what risks are excluded and how much it will cost to broaden your coverage to include them.

> # MYTH
> *"The government will save me."*
>
> ...
>
> **REALITY**
> The average FEMA disaster grant is $5,000.

Many policyholders believe that if there is a major disaster that "the government will take care of me." This is just not true. FEMA sometimes provides grants to help low-income residents re-build but their individual assistance grants are limited to $33,000 per household, and the average is under $5,000 per household. Low interest SBA loans may be made available up to $200,000 but these loans need to be repaid. Other than a loan, your home insurance and savings are the only sources of funding you can count on in the event your home is damaged or destroyed.

What about flood insurance?

If you live near water or an area that's prone to flooding or mudslides, you should buy it if you can afford it, even if your lender is not requiring you to do so. There are official flood zones throughout the United States that have been mapped by the Federal Emergency Management Agency as low to high risk. If you live in a high risk zone and have a mortgage, you have no choice - you must buy flood insurance. The cost will depend on your zone and whether your community participates in a national flood control program.

Options for buying flood insurance are:

- The National Flood Insurance Program. Max coverage is $250k. For more info or to find an agent who sells NFIP policies, visit, www.floodsmart.gov.

- A "high end" home policy that does not exclude flood damage, (Chubb and AIG for example)

- A policy from a Lloyds of London or other surplus lines insurer.

Consider:

- Just because your area hasn't flooded in the past doesn't mean it won't in the future

- Flood maps get outdated and may not be accurate.

- Make sure your contents are also insured. That costs extra.

- There are many limits to NFIP policies, but the policies are backed by the Federal Government.

- Surplus lines policies, such as Lloyds, may offer broader coverage but without that backing and with less regulation.

- Experts predict increased flooding due to climate change.

- Ask your agent if a "DIC" (difference in conditions) policy makes sense for you as a gap filler.

The Big One and the Big Question: "Should I buy earthquake insurance?"

The decision is an individual financial choice best made through three steps:

STEP 1: Know your risk. Could a severe earthquake occur where you live and damage or destroy your home and possessions?

STEP 2: Know your options: Who will sell you earthquake insurance, on what terms, and at what price?

STEP 3: Decide: Should you carry all the risk of paying for repairs yourself or transfer some of that risk to an insurance company?

Questions to ask:

- What is the age and construction style of your home (e.g. does it have a "soft story" living space over a garage)?
- Is your home built or strengthened to withstand shaking during an earthquake?
- What are the soil conditions? (Sand, Fill, Bedrock?)
- How close is your home is to an active fault?
- How much equity do you have in your home?
- Will you be able to finance repairs out of pocket or qualify for a loan if you "go bare"?
- What is the cost of available earthquake insurance options?
- Does a 10% or 15% deductible make more sense?

9 **GET A CLUE**—Before you start shopping for home insurance, spend $8 to get a copy of your "CLUE" report. CLUE (Comprehensive Loss and Underwriting Exchange) is a giant national database of people's insurance claim histories. Insurance companies share their claim data in CLUE and use it to price policies. Your CLUE report is a lot like a credit report. Insurers use it to rate you as a risk—this impacts how much they charge you for insurance:

> **FIXING ERRORS ON YOUR CLUE REPORT** will help you avoid over-paying for your home and car insurance.

If you find errors on your report, get them fixed. For example, you might see on your CLUE report that when you called in to ask a question, it got mis-reported as a claim.

10 **CHOOSE YOUR DEDUCTIBLES**—A higher deductible should lower your premium but is a trade-off. The higher your deductible, the more you'll pay out of pocket in the event of a loss and claim. Ask your agent to explain what kind of deductible choices you have and to give you quotes at various levels of deductibles. Compare the savings and consider whether you'll have cash on hand to cover smaller losses out of pocket. Will the deductible apply to your personal property and loss of use benefits, or are those covered "first dollar"?

11 **DEVILISH DETAILS: EXCLUSIONS, LIMITS, ENDORSEMENTS AND RIDERS**—Home policies contain *exclusions* for certain causes of loss and *limits* for

> **THE (SOFT) STORY: A GARAGE UNDER A HOME** is known as a "soft story" because it lacks structural support in the middle of the room. Pre-1979 homes may also be deemed higher risk for earthquake damage because they were built to building codes that didn't adequately address seismic risks.

certain types of property. In addition to flood, earthquake and earth movement damage, coverage for causes of loss that are often excluded or limited in a home policy include water leaks, sewer and drain backups, mold damage and home-based businesses. When shopping, compare risks that are excluded or limited, and whether you can or should pay extra to cover them.

As explained above, "sub-limits" in addition to your overall policy limits typically apply to jewelry, art, silver, antiques, collectibles, cash, electronic equipment and property or equipment used for business purposes. If you have valuables in these categories, consider buying *endorsements* or *riders* for increased protection.

Some policies will only pay ACV for roofs 10 years or older. Better policies provide replacement value coverage regardless of the roof's age.

The least expensive policy most insurers sell is based on a standardized insurance industry form called an "HO3." For superior coverage, buy an "HO5" policy.

12 "PERSONAL LIABILITY" (COVERAGE E) INSURANCE IS FOR LAWSUITS AND INJURIES—

S#!t happens. If you own a home, your policy should include personal liability coverage to protect it and your other assets in the event of an injury on or near your property, or in a non-vehicle accident anywhere in the world. For example, if you or family members cause an injury (e.g. by hitting someone with a golf ball or hosting

IF YOU REGULARLY EARN MONEY BY RENTING OUT YOUR PROPERTY short or long term through an agency, classified ad service or website such as AirBnB, be aware of the "commercial pursuits" exclusion in many home insurance policies. This exclusion may leave you uninsured for a claim by or related to a renter.

a party where a guest slips on a spilled drink and breaks a leg) you could be liable for the injured person's long-term medical costs, loss of income, etc., plus legal fees to defend yourself. When s#!t happens, you'll be very glad you have liability insurance.

Your liability limits should be high enough to protect your assets (property, savings, etc.) and future earnings. Costs due to injuries and lawsuit costs and lawyer fees can be very substantial and unpredictable. There is often only a small cost difference for buying higher liability limits so why gamble? You may also want to supplement the limits in your home and auto policies by buying an *umbrella* or *personal excess liability* policy (see Chapter 5, Umbrella Policies for more information).

13 INVENTORY YOUR PROPERTY—If you ever need to file a claim it is very helpful to have records and detailed pre-loss documentation of your home and its contents. The better proof you have of your property before the loss, the better positioned you will be to get a fair and prompt insurance settlement. Create an inventory. Your inventory, photographs, blueprints and receipts should be stored off-site or online via cloud storage so that in the event of a fire or other calamity they can be easily accessed.

A very useful tool for this purpose is UP's free App, the *UPHelp Home Inventory*. The app works on smartphones and tablets and is an easy and fast way to document your property with photos and securely store the records so they can be accessed through the web on any computer. Using the app, you can quickly build a complete inventory including

The UpHelp App makes inventorying a snap!

furnishings, artwork, jewelry, appliances, electronics, music, video and book collections and the features of your home. The app is available for iOS and Android through the iTunes Store and the Google Play Store. More information about the *UP Help Home Inventory* app can be found at www.uphelp.org. UP also offers a free home inventory spreadsheet in *Excel* if you prefer to create your own inventory that way.

14 HOUSE KEEPING: BE PROACTIVE IN REDUCING RISK— The following steps will make it less likely that you'll experience a serious or total loss:

• Regularly clear brush and debris from around your home/ structures on all sides.

• Install and maintain smoke alarms.

• In earthquake-prone zones strap your water heater to keep it from falling over, bolt large and heavy bookcases and other furniture to studs in the wall, install seismic bracing, and bolt your home to its foundation.

• Install attic vent screens to keep out flying embers from a wildfire.

• In hurricane and tornado-prone areas, secure roofs and install storm shutters.

• Replace shake/wood roofs with composition or tile.

• Maintain your roof and keep gutters clear.

• Have your chimney cleaned regularly if you use it often.

• Use sandbags to prevent heavy rains from getting inside your home.

• Install flood vents to reduce the cost of flood insurance.

Keeping your home insurance up to date

Your insurer or agent should review your insurance limits with you once a year. Don't ignore recommendations to adjust your coverage to keep your protection current, especially when life changes occur. It's a good idea to check in with your insurer:

> **After a remodel or major repair:** If you are planning additions, major repairs or a remodel, let your insurance company know. You may need to adjust the policy limits. Keep copies of blueprints, construction invoices, receipts for major appliances and other evidence of the work off-site. Get proof of your contractor's general liability and workers compensation insurance so you know where to file a claim if necessary.

DONT GAMBLE: Most insurers require you to notify them if you make improvements that cost more than $5k or that increase the value of your home by 5% or more. If you don't, the improvement may not be covered in the event of a loss.

> **When someone moves into your house:** If someone moves into your house and they are not a dependent and/or are not related to you, you may want to add them to your policy so your liability insurance covers them. For example, if you live with a partner but are not legally married, the partner will have neither personal liability coverage nor any coverage for their stuff unless you add them to the policy.

> **When you acquire or sell high value assets:** Talk with your agent about insuring your fine art, jewelry, musical instruments, collectibles or other assets.

> **When you buy or assume ownership of a new property:** If you buy or inherit a second home or income property, or someone transfers property to your name, you'll want to ensure that you have appropriate property AND liability coverage in place.

> **When your home is transferred to a trust or to one or more of your adult children for estate planning purposes:** The "new owner", including a trust, needs to be named on the home policy and any umbrella policies for the coverage to be valid.

> **When you get engaged or married:** Ask if your home policy covers engagement and wedding rings and wedding gifts. If the fiancé lives alone or with parents, the ring may not be covered under their policy unless a specific endorsement is in place. And if you live together before you officially tie the knot, both spouses names need to be on the home policy so personal liability and personal assets are insured.

> **When you separate or get a divorce:** Keep the home policy in force and in both names until the divorce is final and, if the home is being sold, until the sale is final. Be sure to obtain additional home or renters coverage if one spouse moves to a new house or apartment.

> **When you sign a contract:** Contracts often contain language whereby you agree to "indemnify" someone for any losses or injuries they incur as a result of providing a service to you. By signing a contract, you may be assuming the responsibility to cover the full cost of any losses or injuries that occur for any reason. This gets tricky, but you should always be on the lookout for this kind of language in a contract and when in doubt ask questions or consult

with an attorney. Since you probably won't read the small print or consult with an attorney every time, it's a good idea to have a home and umbrella policy that covers this kind of risk.

❯ **When you get a dog and your policy does not cover the breed:** Typically excluded breeds include Pit Bulls, German Shepherds, Doberman Pinschers, Rottweiler and Siberian Huskies. You may need to add an endorsement on your policy or buy separate dog owner liability insurance.

❯ **When you go on an extended vacation or leave your house empty for over a month:** A "vacancy exclusion" in many policies kicks in when the home is unoccupied for a long period of time.

❯ **When you rent your home out for short-term vacation rentals via Air bnb, VRBO or a similar service:** Be aware that there is an exclusion in almost every residential policy for losses due to "commercial pursuits." Look into buying a rider or policy that will cover you, or check with the listing service about their insurance for hosts.

? **QUESTIONS TO ASK ...**
   When Buying a Home Policy

☐ How much per square foot will my home be insured for?

_____

_____

☐ Will this policy be adequate if I have a total loss?

_____

_____

Will it cover the cost of rebuilding my home to its pre-loss condition, including demolition, debris removal and replacement of the foundation, roof, electrical and plumbing to current codes?

_____

_____

☐ What causes of loss are not covered?

_____

_____

☐ What items are subject to limits or exclusions and for which of these limits or exclusions should I consider adding coverage?

_____

_____

☐ How much can I save if I increase my deductible? Is there more than one deductible in the policy? Is the deductible waived if there is a large loss?

_____

_____

☐ Is my personal property covered for Replacement or Actual Cash Value? If replacement value is not included, what would it cost to add this coverage?

_____

_____

☐ Will my insurance cover the cost to upgrade electrical, plumbing and other systems if I have to make repairs after a loss?

_____

_____

☐ For how long will my temporary rent and related expenses be covered while my home is being repaired or rebuilt after a loss? Is there a total dollar cap, monthly cap or time limit on this coverage?

_____

_____

☐ Is my Coverage E (Personal Liability) limit enough to protect my assets and future income? If not, what does umbrella coverage cost?

_____

_____

☐ What discounts are available?

_____

_____

☐ Will this policy cover all of the residents of my household even if they are not legally related or do I need to add their names to the policy?

_____

_____

☐ If someone sues me, will my liability coverage pay for legal fees?

_____

_____

☐ Do I have enough coverage to replace my unique or special items such as electronics, piano, jewelry, fine art, oriental rugs, wine, collectibles, etc.?

_____

_____

☐ What are my options for insuring my home-based business property and operations?

_____

_____

☐ If only a part of my roof or siding gets damaged, will this policy pay to replace all the shingles or siding so it matches?

_____

_____

☐ Does the age of my roof matter?

_____

_____

☐ Does this policy exclude or cap coverage for mold damage? What about water damage?

_____

_____

☐ What are this insurance company's rules for premium increases and non-renewals if I file a claim?

_____

_____

Renters Insurance

What is renters insurance?

Standard renters insurance covers your belongings from theft, fire and, in some cases, water damage, plus loss of use (moving costs and alternate housing if your place becomes uninhabitable). It also protects you if an accident or injury occurs at the rented property or is caused by you (the renter). Standard renters policies do not cover damage caused by earthquake or flood. You can add that coverage with a separate policy or an add-on "endorsement" or "rider".

Why buy renters insurance?

If you are a renter with assets of $10,000 or higher, UP recommends buying renters insurance. If your apartment or house gets burglarized, or damaged or destroyed by a fire or other calamity, renters insurance pays benefits to replace your personal property and help you relocate if need be. If you live in a rent-controlled unit or a city where rental units are in high demand and short supply, renters insurance should help you relocate even if your only option is a more expensive place.

If you accidentally cause a fire that damages the

A DAY IN
The (Real) Life

You're a renter in an apartment in an older building. You host a party to celebrate your new job. It's a warm evening so people gather outside on the deck. The landlord has not been maintaining the building. The weight causes the deck to collapse, sending 10 people to the hospital with serious injuries. Even though it wasn't your fault, the injured people sue you to get their losses covered. Without liability insurance, there's a good chance your savings will be wiped out and your wages will be garnished for a very very long time. And good luck renting or buying in the future...

building, most renters policies will pay for the damage, up to the policy limits. Some landlords require their tenants to have renters insurance. Renters insurance protects you and family members if someone sues you after an accident or injury. Renters insurance is a bargain compared to most kinds of insurance.

A SECTION 8 TENANT (whose rent is subsidized by government programs) cannot legally be required to buy renters insurance But according to the American Red Cross, renters insurance can prevent homelessness after apartment fires and other catastrophes.

Things to consider when buying renters insurance

1 **AIM FOR REPLACEMENT COST (RC) COVERAGE NOT ACTUAL CASH VALUE COVERAGE (ACV)**—These are the two types of coverage for personal property—RC is better, ACV is cheaper. If you have RC coverage, your insurance company will reimburse you for the actual cost of replacing what you lost. If you only have ACV, your insurance company will only pay what a willing buyer would have paid you immediately before the loss based on the items. UP *strongly* recommends buying replacement cost coverage if you can afford it.

2 **WHAT ARE YOUR LOCAL RISKS?**—If you are in an earthquake zone or a ground floor unit in a flood zone, you need a separate policy or rider to cover those risks.

3 **CREATE A BASIC INVENTORY**—Start with the most valuable items. A convenient time to do this is when you are packing or unpacking for a move. The inventory will help you decide what kind of limits you need to buy and will be a big help if you ever need to file a claim. The *UPHelp Home Inventory* App (a free download at the iTunes Store and Google Play Store) will make it quick and easy for you to create an inventory and store it securely online.

4 CUSTOMIZE YOUR SAFETY NET—A standard renters policy has caps/limits on payments for certain items such as business equipment, jewelry and electronics. If you work from home, and/or have collections, art or high value items, consider buying extra coverage or "scheduling" (listing) those items.

5 YOUR PERSONAL LIABILITY LIMITS SHOULD COVER YOUR ASSETS AND FUTURE EARNINGS—Your renters policy should protect you in the event of an injury on or near your property, but also for non-vehicle-related accidents anywhere in the world. If you or a family member who lives with you causes an injury (e.g. by getting into a fight or throwing a baseball) you could be liable for long-term medical and related costs such as the injured person's loss of income.

Consider the amount of your assets (savings, earnings, valuables, etc.) that could be tapped in a worst-case scenario. Include future earnings that could be garnished. Buy adequate or higher liability limits. There is often little cost difference to increase these limits. You can also supplement the limits in your renters and auto policies by buying an *umbrella* that provides higher limits.

6 SHOP AROUND—Use the UP Shopping Guide for Renters Insurance, search the Internet, call toll-free numbers, compare what competing insurance companies offer. If there's a local agent that advertises renters insurance, give him or her a call.

7 ASK FOR DISCOUNTS—Don't wait for insurers to offer. Most insurance companies will give you a discount for buying your renters and car insurance from them. Discounts are available for having an alarm system, clean claim history and/or good credit score.

8 CHOOSE YOUR DEDUCTIBLE—A deductible is the amount of a claim or loss that you are responsible for before the insurance company's obligation to pay kicks in. Opting for a higher deductible in any policy lowers your premium, but with renters insurance not so much because renters insurance premiums are low to begin with. So unlike a home policy, it may not make sense to carry a higher deductible on a renters policy. $500 is common.

Keeping your renters insurance up to date

Once you have the right insurance in place, your insurer should review it once a year with you to make sure your coverage matches your current situation as life changes occur. Some of these changes include:

> **SOMEONE MOVES INTO YOUR HOME**—If someone moves into your home and they are not a dependent or legally related to you, consider adding them as an insured on your renters policy, or encourage them to buy their own insurance.

> **YOU GET ENGAGED OR MARRIED**—Ask if your home policy covers engagement rings, wedding rings and wedding gifts. If the fiancé lives alone or with parents, the ring may not be covered unless a specific endorsement is in place. And if you live together before you tie the knot, both names need to be on the renters policy for personal liability and personal assets to be insured.

> **YOU ACQUIRE ASSETS**—New electronics, musical instruments, art, jewelry, collectibles or other assets may need to be specifically added to your policy.

> **YOU SEPARATE OR GET A DIVORCE**—Keep your renters policy in place and in both names until the divorce is final. Be sure to obtain additional renters coverage if one spouse moves to a new house or apartment.

❯ **YOU'RE HOSTING A LARGE PARTY OR EVENT AT YOUR RENTAL HOME**—Consider buying a special policy for the event.

❯ **YOU CO-SIGN A LEASE**—If you co-sign a lease for someone they may or may not automatically be covered under your renters policy unless you specifically add them by name.

❯ **YOU GET A DOG AND YOUR POLICY DOES NOT COVER THE BREED**—Typically excluded breeds include Pit Bulls, German Shepherds, Doberman Pinschers, Rottweilers and Siberian Huskies. If your breed is excluded you need to pay for an endorsement to your policy or buy separate dog owner liability insurance.

❯ **YOU RENT YOUR HOME OUT FOR SHORT-TERM VACATION RENTALS VIA ADS, AIR BNB, VRBO OR A SIMILAR SERVICE**—The "commercial pursuits" exclusion in virtually every renters policy can leave you unprotected if a loss or accident occurs during a rental. Look into buying a rider or policy that will cover you, or check with the listing service about their insurance for hosts.

? QUESTIONS TO ASK ...
When Buying A Renters Policy

☐ Will this policy cover the cost of repairing or replacing my personal property and relocating me if the home or apartment I am renting is damaged or destroyed in a fire, earthquake, hurricane or flood?

_____

_____

☐ What risks are not covered and should I add coverage for them?

_____

_____

☐ For how long will my temporary rent and relocation expenses be covered after a loss?

_____

_____

☐ Is there a total dollar cap, monthly cap or time limit on temporary rent coverage?

_____

_____

☐ Do benefits stop once I've relocated?

_____

_____

☐ What if my new rent is higher?

_____

_____

☐ Will this policy allow me to replace my unique or special possessions such as electronics, musical instruments, jewelry, fine art, wine, collectibles, etc.?

_____

_____

☐ Is my personal property coverage for Replacement or only Actual Cost Value? If replacement value is not included, what would be the cost to upgrade from Actual Cost Value?

_____

_____

☐ Is my personal liability limit adequate to protect my assets? If not, what does umbrella coverage cost?

_____

_____

☐ Will this policy cover all of the residents of my household even if they are not legally related or do I need to add their names to the policy?

_____

_____

☐ How much can I save by increasing my deductible?

_____

_____

☐ What are this insurance company's rules for premium increases and non-renewals if I file a claim?

_____

_____

Auto Insurance

What is auto insurance?

Auto insurance pays benefits to repair or replace a vehicle that gets damaged, stolen or destroyed. It also provides *bodily injury* and *liability* protection to cover harm to other people, other vehicles and property. Liability protection is what you need if you're involved in an accident resulting in property damage, injuries or death, legal matters, and related obligations. Auto insurance should also include *Medical Expense Coverage* or *Personal Injury Protection* for medical expenses and to compensate occupants of your vehicle if they are injured.

In every state but New Hampshire, the law requires you to carry insurance if you're driving a car. In many states, your policy has to include *Uninsured and Underinsured Motorist Coverage, UM/ UIM.* This coverage protects you and your passengers for an accident with a driver who has too little or no insurance. Experts say that at a busy intersection in a typical city, 1 out of 10 drivers are uninsured. Even if your state doesn't require it, UP highly recommends buying UM/UIM coverage.

Depending on the company you're insured with, your policy can also include coverage for a rental car while yours is being repaired, roadside assistance, windshield crack repair and coverage for vehicles you rent while on vacation or a business trip.

If you don't own a car but are regularly renting, borrowing or casual car-pooling with people you don't know, consider buying a *non-owner auto policy.* They can be a very affordable and practical buy.

If you're using your car to earn money through the "sharing economy" as a driver for Uber, Lyft or other ride-sharing service and you're using an app to connect with riders/customers, be aware that your auto policy most likely contains a *"commercial pursuits" exclusion.* This exclusion can leave you without an insurance safety net if you hit someone or something or are in an accident while the app is on. For more info see Auto Insurance Basics for Ridesharing Drivers at uphelp.org. Coverage may be available through the ride-sharing company that hosts the app or new policies that are becoming available in some parts of the U.S. for this specific risk (using your personal auto for commercial purposes).

Why buy auto insurance?

If you drive a car (your own, or one that's borrowed, rented or leased) you buy auto insurance to protect yourself, your loved ones and your assets, and to comply with the law. Virtually every state requires you to have insurance in order to legally drive a car. In addition to complying with the laws in your state, you should carry enough insurance to:

1. Protect yourself in the event of an accident or injury you cause (or someone accuses you of causing).

2. Protect yourself if an uninsured or underinsured motorist injures you.

3. Cover the repair or replacement of your vehicle.

Coverage categories

COLLISION—Covers damage to your vehicle from hitting another vehicle or object.

COMPREHENSIVE—Covers most other kinds of accidental damage to your vehicle, such as fire, flood, theft, vandalism, glass breakage, hail or wind damage.

LOSS OF USE—Can cover taxi fare and the cost of renting a vehicle while your car is being repaired for a covered loss. See also "Rental Car Coverage."

LIABILITY—Covers injuries and damage to other cars, individuals and property if you are found to be at fault. The limits of your liability coverage are usually listed as three numbers (for example: 25/50/25). These numbers represent, in thousands, the amount of available coverage in three categories: The first is the maximum the policy will pay for *each* person that suffers bodily injury in an accident ($25,000). The second is the overall maximum the policy will pay for *all* persons who suffer bodily injury in an accident ($50,000). The third is the maximum the policy will pay for property damage per accident ($25,000). Bodily injury costs may include medical bills, loss of income, and loss of the enjoyment of life, loss of earning capacity and other damages allowed by law. Sometimes liability limits are a "combined single limit" that applies to both bodily injury and property damage per incident.

MEDICAL PAYMENTS—Covers medical costs for you and your passengers, and in some cases for injured pedestrians, regardless of fault. In some states, medical expense coverage is called Personal Injury Protection or "PIP". In some cases, related costs such as loss of income, childcare expenses and funeral costs are also covered. In some states, motorists are required to have medical expense or PIP coverage.

UNINSURED AND UNDERINSURED MOTORIST—Covers your medical costs, lost wages and other injury-related expenses where the motorist at fault is uninsured or underinsured, or if you are injured by a stolen vehicle or in a hit-and-run. The term "Uninsured Motorist Coverage" is often used to refer to both Uninsured and Underinsured Motorist Coverage.

ROADSIDE ASSISTANCE—Covers costs related to emergency roadside assistance and towing.

RENTAL CAR COVERAGE—Covers the cost of a rental while your car is being repaired. See also "Loss of Use."

Things to consider when buying auto insurance

1 **DECIDE WHETHER YOU NEED COLLISION AND COMPREHENSIVE COVERAGE**—If you own a high value car or one that is financed by a loan or lease, then collision and comprehensive coverage make sense (or may be required by the financing company). If you drive an older or dinged-up car, you may want to forego these two options to avoid paying out more in premiums over time than the car is worth.

AS A RULE OF THUMB, divide your car's replacement value by 5 and compare it to cost quotes for collision and comprehensive coverage. If the cost of coverage is higher, you might want to skip those coverage options and focus on paying for adequate liability and uninsured motorist coverage.

2 **BUY ENOUGH LIABILITY AND UNINSURED MOTORIST COVERAGE**—A common mistake people make when buying car insurance is buying too little *liability* and/or *uninsured motorist* coverage. The condition and value of your car should have no bearing on the amount of your liability insurance. Even if you are driving an old "clunker," you still need adequate liability and uninsured motorist coverage to protect your assets.

If you cause an accident with injuries and/or property damage higher than your coverage limits you may have to cover the gap out of your own pocket. A single auto accident can wipe you out financially if your insurance is not adequate. Your wages can be garnished and your savings can be seized.

Turn the tables on "price-optimizing" insurers: Shop and compare

The phrase "price optimization" is hot in the insurance world, probably invented by an MBA genius. It basically means, "charge as much as you can get away with before losing a customer to a competitor," and it's linked to data mining and predictive analytics.

Insurance companies are now data mining and learning all about your shopping, eating, and financial habits, which helps them figure out how high they can raise your rates before you will switch to another insurer. And by advertising loyalty discounts, they discourage you from switching.

We're not convinced that loyalty discounts are all that. The only way to get the best price and quality auto insurance is to shop and compare. Do a little price optimizing yourself to figure out how little you can pay for the coverage you need.

Most states require you to buy *some* liability and uninsured motorist coverage, but the mandatory minimum limits are low, and have not kept up with inflation. For example, California law requires liability limits of 15/30/5, which means only $15k for medical costs per individual, $30k for medical costs per accident and $5k for property damage. These numbers are way too low and out of date. The truth is, medical expenses add up fast and can include doctor bills *plus* lost wages, pain and suffering, etc.

We recommend buying adequate liability *and* uninsured/underinsured motorist coverage. UM/UIM coverage protects you and passengers in your vehicle if someone who carries little or no insurance hits you. In some states, 40% of drivers fall into this category. *This coverage is especially important if you carry other people's children in your car.*

3 **COMPARE, COMPARE, COMPARE**—Unless you have a bad driving record, chances are there are lots of companies competing to sell you auto insurance. Use that to your advantage by asking the right questions and comparing options.

Insurance companies advertise like crazy and compete for your business by claiming that their rates are lower than their competitors. But just as with home insurance, the *quality* of your coverage matters. If you have assets to protect, buy the car policy that will cover you, your car *and* your assets. Don't skimp unless you have no choice.

Auto insurance companies use many factors to quote you a price for car insurance: Your home address/principal place of garaging, the model and year of your car, your driving record, CLUE report, shopping habits, age and in most states…credit score. Each insurer uses its own formulas for deciding what kind of risk you are and how much they will charge you. By getting quotes from two or three different insurers you can take advantage of competition and save money.

4 **CHOOSE THE RIGHT DEDUCTIBLE**—Consumer advocates generally agree that opting for higher insurance deductibles makes good economic sense. Why? Every claim you file can put you in a higher risk category and increase the cost of your insurance. Filing small claims you can afford to pay out of pocket isn't financially wise and a policy with a higher deductible is cheaper than one with a lower deductible.

Get quotes based on different deductible amounts then decide which is right for you. If you can afford to pay repairs or damage below $1000 then setting your deductible at $1000 (instead of $500 or $300) makes sense. If you assume that a claim will occur once every five years or so, multiply the premium savings by 5 and if it equals the difference in the deductible amount, and you can afford to pay it, then opt for the higher deductible.

5 **SHOULD YOU BUY MEDICAL EXPENSE OR PIP COVERAGE?**— Medical expense coverage is inexpensive and protects you and other passengers in your vehicle by providing "no-fault" coverage for basic injuries so you don't have to file a lawsuit to get expenses paid. If money is tight and you already have good health coverage, you may not need additional medical coverage other than for co-pays. Get a quote for Medical Payments coverage and consider whether or not your medical plan has high co-pays and how often passengers who are not covered by your health plan ride with you.

6 **BUY THE SAME LIMIT/AMOUNT OF UNINSURED MOTORIST COVERAGE AND AUTO LIABILITY COVERAGE AS YOU HAVE IN YOUR HOME AND UMBRELLA POLICY**—If you carry a $1M liability limit on your home or renters policy, buy the same limit for your auto liability and uninsured motorist coverage. Higher limits can be added at a reasonable cost that may surprise you. This is because the higher the limits go, the lower likelihood of payout is reflected in the premium cost, so you can add a lot of protection without spending a lot of money. If you have a good umbrella policy that covers liability above your home policy limits, you'll want to be sure the liability limit in your auto policy matches up so there is no gap in coverage. If your assets are modest, you don't need to spend on enhanced liability protection.

7 **ASK ABOUT OEM PARTS AND BODY SHOP SELECTION**—Some insurance companies save money for themselves on repairs by specifying that collision repairs will be done with "aftermarket," used or non-OEM parts. OEM (original equipment manufacturer) parts can cost significantly more than aftermarket/generic or "crash" parts. If you want repairs done with OEM parts, this is something you should ask about when you buy auto insurance.

Many manufacturers will void their warranties if OEM parts are not used, and OEM parts generally preserve your car's resale value.

When shopping for auto insurance, it's a good idea to ask your agent whether there are limits or restrictions on replacement parts, repair methods and/or body shop selection.

8 BE SAVVY WHEN INSURING SPOUSES AND CHILDREN—If there are multiple drivers and cars of different ages in your household, you can put everyone on one policy or buy separate policies. Insurers consider the age, address and record of the driver, the make, model and age of the car and whether it is garaged or parked on the street when pricing an auto policy. There are many other factors insurers consider, depending on the state. Purchasing separate policies for new or "high-risk" drivers in your household *may* be less expensive than having everyone on one policy. Get quotes and compare.

When your teen gets his/her learner's permit, check with your insurer. Most will automatically cover them without a premium increase until they get their full license.

9 ROADSIDE ASSISTANCE COVERAGE—You won't need this if you are already covered by your auto manufacturer or an Auto Club. If you are considering adding it to your auto policy, ask about the rules (e.g. How far a tow can you get? Can you get a replacement for a dead battery?) to figure out if it is worth the cost.

10 Discounts—Don't wait for an offer. Ask about and get all of the discounts you are eligible for. They can include:

- Customer loyalty ("a persistence discount")
- Bundling your home or renters and auto policies with one insurer.
- Good driver
- Good credit score
- Good school grades
- Age

- Completing a safe driving course
- Safety equipment (anti-lock brakes, etc.)
- Miles driven (fewer is better)
- Electric vehicle or hybrid
- Affiliations (military, Federal employee, credit unions, alumni associations, professional memberships)

11 SELLING YOUR CAR—When you sell your car, make sure the sale is properly documented to transfer the title to the new owner. Once that's completed, cancel your insurance. This process varies by state, so you may want to check the website of your state's Department of Motor Vehicles for instructions. Don't rely on the new owner to process the paperwork. If they fail to do so and the car is involved in an accident before title is legally transferred, you could be financially responsible for the damages.

12 BUYING AUTO INSURANCE ONLINE—It's becoming more and more common for people to bypass an agent or broker and buy their car insurance online or through a toll free number.

If you're bypassing the expertise you get from an experienced agent or broker, it's extra important to do your homework and tailor your policy to meet your protection goals.

See the "Questions to Ask…" section below, and *buy enough liability and UM/UIM coverage to protect you and your family from catastrophic financial losses.* Online quotes are usually based on the minimum required liability limits in your state. That may not be high enough to protect you and your level of assets.

Insuring a rental car

CDW OR NOT? If you've rented a car, chances are your pen has hovered over the boxes in the rental contract while you ponder: "Should I or shouldn't I buy the Collision Damage Waiver ("CDW")? Geez—if I pay for the insurance, I lose the bargain rental rate. Maybe my car insurance will cover me."

Indeed, the fees for buying insurance from a rental car company can exceed the cost of renting the car. There's no point wasting money if you've got coverage through your personal or business policy. But it's scary to decline the coverage if you're not sure. After all, you'll be driving an unfamiliar car, most likely in an unfamiliar place—which can increase the risk of an accident. Credit cards and employer policies often offer this coverage. So are you covered or not?

Your personal policy probably covers cars you rent for casual use, and you can confirm that with a phone call to your insurer. Renting a car for business travel is another story. Most personal policies contain a "commercial pursuits" exclusion that could trip you up on coverage. Coverage for rental vehicles under your personal policy is typically restricted to 21 days, so if you're doing a long-term rental, you will need extra coverage.

To be on the safe side, get the scoop directly from your insurer or agent before making your decision on whether or not to buy insurance through the rental agency.

RENTAL CAR LIABILITY VS. PROPERTY DAMAGE COVERAGE. If you do buy a collision damage waiver or "regular" insurance from a car rental company, it probably contains exclusions you won't see in a typical personal auto policy. For example, some policies exclude coverage for a claim if someone other than the listed driver is driving, if you are driving in a "careless manner" or if you drive after drinking any alcohol whatsoever.

Because auto policies and state laws differ widely, ask your insurer or agent how your current auto and umbrella policies apply to rental vehicles and what kind of limits, restrictions and deductibles apply. Ask whether your auto policy covers rental cars in the US and Canada. Ask if it applies to vehicles rented abroad.

If you are driving a rented vehicle in the US, your personal auto policy will usually cover *liability* for injuries and property damage that you cause as a driver. Your personal auto policy should cover you up to your auto liability limit. If you also have an umbrella policy it should cover additional liability up to your umbrella limit.

If your current personal auto policy includes *Collision and Comprehensive* coverage, then you are probably covered for these same risks when driving a rental car but the coverage could be limited to the value of your own vehicle, leaving you short if the rental car is of higher value.

If you don't own a car or aren't sure your policy will protect you when driving a rental, then UP recommends that you buy both liability and collision damage waiver coverage from the rental agency. If there will be other people driving the rental car, they also need to be listed on the rental form to be covered.

If you are renting a car outside the U.S., UP recommends that you bite the bullet and pay for all available coverage including liability and damage to the rental car. The one exception to this rule is if you have a personal umbrella policy that covers global liability. While your auto policy is likely limited to covering rentals in the U.S., your umbrella policy is probably global. Again, ask your insurance company what your umbrella policy covers when you are renting a vehicle abroad so you can decide if you need extra coverage.

Even if you do have automatic coverage under your current auto policy, you still might want to purchase CDW coverage when renting a car to avoid an increase in your insurance rates as a result of filing a claim, especially if you have a poor driving record or recent claims.

CREDIT CARDS—Some credit cards provide insurance coverage when the card is used to pay for the rental car and the driver on the rental contract is the driver on the credit card. **In most cases the coverage a credit card gives you is limited to damage to the rental vehicle and does not include any form of liability coverage.** The quality of this coverage varies widely, so if you want to rely on it, get a copy of the policy language from your credit card company and ask your insurance agent to read it and advise you.

BUSINESS TRAVEL—If you are renting a car for business, follow your employer's guidelines. Some companies have arrangements with rental agencies that include coverage and pre-negotiated rental rates. Some employers carry auto insurance that covers rental cars used for company business. Others issue company credit cards that may

---

MIND THE GAP— GAP INSURANCE ON A FINANCED CAR

If you're buying a car on credit, especially with low money down, you may want or be required to buy "GAP" (Guaranteed Asset Protection) insurance.

This type of insurance protects you if the value of your damaged car at the time of an accident is less than your loan balance. Cars depreciate fairly quickly, but finance charges and car loans take time to pay down so this is a real risk.

You'll pay less for GAP insurance if you buy it from an insurance company and not through a car dealer.

provide coverage. If you're unsure or your company doesn't have a commercial auto policy, or you're self-employed, it is a good idea to buy all optional coverage when you rent a car. This will prevent you from having to make a claim on your own personal auto insurance that can put you in a higher risk category and lead to your paying more for your insurance.

THE BOTTOM LINE: buying CDW or equivalent insurance from a rental car agency will avoid hassles and gaps if the rental vehicle is damaged, especially when traveling overseas, but for short term domestic rentals for personal/vacation use, your personal auto policy plus the protection that comes with most credit cards is generally adequate.

? **QUESTIONS TO ASK ...**
  When Buying An Auto Policy

☐ Is it worth buying Collision and/or Comprehensive coverage for my current car?

_____

_____

☐ How much can I save by increasing my deductible?

_____

_____

☐ Do I have enough Uninsured and Underinsured Motorist coverage?

_____

_____

☐ Do I have coverage for a rental car while my car is in the shop for repairs?

_____

_____

☐ I want liability limits that will protect my assets after a serious accident. Will this policy do that?

_____

_____

☐ Will my policy pay for genuine OEM (Original Equipment Manufacturer) parts or only for cheaper "after-market" or "crash" parts?

_____

_____

☐ Can I select the auto body repair shop of my choice?

_____

_____

☐ Am I getting all the discounts I am eligible for?

_____

_____

☐ For multiple drivers or cars in one household: am I better off insuring all the drivers on one policy, or should I opt for separate policies?

_____

_____

☐ How will you (the insurance company) value my car if it's totaled?

_____

_____

☐ What will happen if I think my car's a total loss but you (the insurance company) don't?

_____

_____

☐ What will my insurance cover if I rent a car and get in an accident?

_____

_____

☐ If I buy this policy, will I still need to pay for CDW and/or liability coverage when renting a car?

_____

_____

☐ What are this insurance company's rules for post-claim rate increases and non-renewals?

_____

_____

Umbrella Insurance

What is umbrella insurance?

Umbrella insurance gives you an extra layer of liability insurance protection on top of your home, renters or auto policies. The main reason for buying it is to protect your assets (home, savings, etc.) in the event of a lawsuit or legal claim involving serious or big dollar injuries. Umbrella coverage (also called "excess liability" insurance) is generally sold in increments of $1 million and in amounts up to $10 million. An umbrella policy makes sense if you have substantial assets to protect.

Why buy umbrella insurance?

An umbrella policy can give you a lot of financial protection for a relatively low price. It comes into play if you're involved in a major auto accident or defamation (slander or libel) claim. Other common sources of liability for which an umbrella would protect you are claims related to your volunteer or charity work or board service, or sports such as golf or baseball where serious injuries can lead to significant expenses and potentially devastating financial consequences.

Things to consider when buying umbrella insurance

1 DO YOU NEED IT?—If you don't own a home or other high value asset, *and* your income is modest, you probably don't need an umbrella policy. If your assets, work and/or hobbies make you a target for a lawsuit, you probably do.

2 **WILL ADDING AN UMBRELLA GIVE ME USEFUL PROTECTION AND A DISCOUNT ON MY HOME/RENTERS/AUTO INSURANCE?**—Since you want all of your policies to work together to protect you without gaps in coverage and you want your insurance to be cost-effective, it's common to buy your umbrella, home or renters and auto policies through one insurance company.

But as discussed earlier, this is not always or automatically the way to get the best coverage at the best price. It may make sense to buy your home and auto policies from different companies, and bundle your umbrella with one of them.

When you're shopping for home and car insurance, there's no harm in getting quotes for all three. If you've already got your car and home insured, you can add an umbrella layer at any time. You don't need to wait until your current policies expire to do this. You are generally entitled to a "pro rata" refund of remaining premium whenever you terminate a home or auto policy to move to a different insurer.

3 **YOUR UMBRELLA POLICY LIMITS SHOULD BE ADEQUATE TO PROTECT YOUR ASSETS AND POTENTIAL FUTURE EARNINGS**—The size of your savings and income affects the probability that you may be sued. The higher your net worth, the more likely it is that you could be sued.

A good rule of thumb is to buy $1 million more of umbrella coverage than you think you will need. This is driven by the relatively low cost of an additional coverage and the benefit of having adequate protection. Remember that you are not only trying to protect the assets and savings you have today, but also your future income and earnings since they could be tapped to cover a legal judgment.

4 **COVER YOUR UNIQUE RISKS**—Are you a public figure, prominent in your community, or a spokesperson in the media? Do you own an exotic pet, a swimming pool or a trampoline? Do you operate a day-care center or serve on a non-profit board of directors? Does anyone in your family play extreme sports, or engage in activities such as hunting or rock climbing? An umbrella policy makes sense if one or more of these scenarios apply to you.

The contracts you sign when you rent someone else's property, vehicle or equipment almost always make you responsible not only for damage to the rented property but also for any injuries or damages that occur during the rental period, plus related legal fees incurred by the rental agency. You may even be responsible for damage resulting from a storm or other "act of God" that causes damage through no fault of your own. A good umbrella policy will cover your exposures related to these kinds of rentals.

WHEN SHOPPING FOR AN UMBRELLA POLICY, ask about coverage restrictions. You wouldn't want to find out after a serious accident in your rented 30' RV that your umbrella policy only covers an RV 29 feet or shorter.

5 **COVER YOUR CONTRACTUAL LIABILITIES**—In Chapter One, we talked about indemnification, which involves you agreeing to cover losses or damages incurred by a third party. One example would be when you sign a contract for a caterer to provide food for a party. The contract may include language whereby you agree to indemnify the caterer for any losses or injuries that occur while the caterer is providing services to you. If the caterer or one of their employees is injured, you may have agreed to pay for medical and related costs when you signed the contract with them. These costs may or may not be covered by your home policy, but in most cases would be covered by your umbrella policy. Be sure to ask the insurer or agent whether or not these kinds of liabilities are covered.

6 **CONSIDER PEACE OF MIND AND MORAL RESPONSIBILITY**—Even if you're not a millionaire, the cost of an umbrella policy can be so reasonable that you may want to buy one just to ensure that you are able to cover medical and related costs of someone you inadvertently injure and/or property damage that you cause. If you accidentally hit a pedestrian, for example, a good umbrella policy could mean the difference between being able or unable to pay the victim's medical bills, lost wages and compensation for pain and suffering. Some people sleep better at night knowing they have this coverage in place.

7 **REVIEW YOUR COVERAGE AT LEAST ANNUALLY**—Once your umbrella policy is in place, at least once a year you should review it and ask yourself:

- Is the umbrella limit adequate to protect my and/or my family's current financial situation?
- Have I or my family been exposed to any new risks and if so, are they covered? (E.g. a new sporting activity, new swimming pool or new trampoline)
- Did I or do I plan to sign any new contracts that could trigger new indemnification liabilities, and if so, are they covered?
- Have I made any changes to the limits in my basic underlying policies that are inconsistent with the requirements of the umbrella policy?

? QUESTIONS TO ASK ...
When Buying An Umbrella Policy

☐ Will this policy protect my and my household members' current assets and future earnings?

_____

_____

☐ How much would it cost to increase the limits by an additional $1 or $2 million?

_____

_____

☐ Will the policy cover all of my unique risk exposures (especially those not covered in my home and auto insurance or my employer's policies)?

_____

_____

☐ Does my basic home/auto/renters policy have the minimum liability limits required by the terms of the umbrella policy?

_____

_____

☐ Will the umbrella policy cover contractual indemnification liabilities that I assume when I sign contracts with rental agencies, caterers and other service providers?

_____

_____

☐ Will the cost of legal defense be covered within the limit of my umbrella liability coverage or in addition to that limit? Are my combined limits adequate to cover both legal defense and settlement costs?

_____

_____

☐ Does the umbrella policy provide additional coverage for uninsured or underinsured motorists above what's covered by my car insurance policy?

_____

_____

☐ Does this policy cover me when I'm driving a rental car?

_____

_____

6

Filing an Insurance Claim

When and when *not* to (use it and lose it)

If you are involved in a car accident, a large house fire or other serious loss event, the first thing to do, after you make sure everyone is safe, is notify your insurance company about the event, and get a complete and current copy of your insurance policy. That's what insurance is for. But for minor, smaller events, in many cases you're better off not using your insurance by filing a claim.

For a bike theft, broken window, or any home repair under $1,000 think things through before filing a claim. Yes it's unfair, but a claim can trigger a premium increase or non-renewal. (For more info on the "use it and lose it" insurance phenomenon, visit www.uphelp.org.)

Thinking "I paid for this insurance, I'm going to use it" and filing a claim may not be the smart move. To figure out if it makes financial sense to file an insurance claim you need to do a bit of math.

REFRAINING FROM CLAIMING? After a car accident involving any other driver or property, you need to notify your insurer. It's too risky not to. The same goes for accidents in your home involving injuries. But for very minor property damage consider paying out of pocket.

CLAIM FILING MATH: Don't file a claim if you're sure the damage is less than your deductible. If it is, you won't recover a dime from your insurer but the claim goes on your record and may put you in a higher risk/rate category—even though you didn't collect any benefits.

If you're not sure how much the damage is—try and figure it out before filing a claim—but don't wait too long. If you wait too long after a loss to notify your insurer—the insurer may complain that you "prejudiced" them by failing to notify them promptly. They may even deny the claim on that basis.

MORE MATH: If the damage is less than a few hundred dollars above your deductible— again—probably not worth filing. Pay it out of pocket. Yes it's unfair to be penalized for using the insurance you've paid for. But because most states allow insurers to freely charge their customers more after they file claims—its up to you to protect yourself. Some states limit the amount an insurer can surcharge you after a claim, but generally, it's a free-for-all.

NOW THE RESEARCH: Ask your agent or insurer point blank—how much will my rate go up if I file one, two or more claims? Does it matter how far apart they occur?

Write down the answers and keep them with your insurance policy for future reference.

NOW YOU CAN MAKE AN EDUCATED DECISION. If damage is well above your deductible—by all means file it. That's why you pay for insurance. If your rate goes up as a result—complain in writing to the insurer, and to your state regulator—and confirm that the increase was legal and consistent with the rating plan they filed with the state.

If you learn that your insurer will penalize you for filing even one claim, consider switching to a more customer-friendly insurance company that has fairer rules. Many insurers will not penalize you for filing just one claim—even if it was your fault.

If you do decide to file an insurance claim, our Top 10 Insurance Claim Tips and online library at uphelp.org offer guidance on how to make sure your claim goes as smoothly as possible.

Top 10 insurance claim tips

1 Visit the Claim Guidance library at uphelp.org to get oriented. Be pro-active and politely assertive in the claim process. Keep a diary from day one in writing or dictated on a smart phone.

2 Think of your insurance claim as a business negotiation—you're dealing with a for-profit company whose settlement objectives are not 100% aligned with yours.

3 Keep in mind that you're not on a level playing field with an insurance claim. You're a rookie, the insurer and adjuster are veterans.

4 Give your insurance company a chance to do the right thing, but don't mistake a friendly claim representative for a friend, or automatically trust an expert your insurer hires.

5 Document and support your claim with proof, details and estimates. Arrange for inspections and reports from independent professionals if you're not in agreement with your insurer about damage or costs.

6 Present clear requests in writing that explain what you need, when you need it, and why you're entitled to it.

7 Don't pad or exaggerate your losses.

8 Don't sign legally binding documents that you don't fully understand.

9 Try to resolve problems informally, but complain in writing, go up the chain of command and/or use government agency help when necessary.

10 Get specialized professional help when you need it, start in the "Find Help" section of www.uphelp.org.

Communicating with your insurance company

Communicating effectively and clearly with your insurance company is very important to successfully settling a claim. The insurance company may try to handle your claim by telephone, with no records. The more severe or complex the damage is, the more likely it will require physical inspections, time and dispute resolution. You *must* make sure everything gets documented in writing. How you communicate makes a world of difference in the amount of benefits you collect and how fast you collect them. The squeaky wheel gets paid.

We recommend that you:

1 **Create a paper trail.** Document conversations and communications in a notebook, diary or recording device so you can keep track of the status of your claim. Confirm representations and promises made in person or over the phone by insurance company personnel by sending them a short follow-up e-mail or letter.

2 **Be professional.** Use good grammar, punctuation and capitalization. Promptly respond to letters and requests if they are reasonable. If they are not, say so, in writing.

3 **Be proactive.** Give your insurer proof of your losses and ask for the dollar amounts you are entitled to. Don't wait for them to tell you how much they owe you.

4 **Get second opinions on damage.** It's best to get 2-3 opinions and estimates from qualified repair pros on the scope and cost of the work that's needed to restore your property to its pre-loss condition.

5 **Summarize the facts that are in your favor and use them as negotiating leverage.** Your diary will come in handy. For example, showing the insurance company proof that it dragged its feet or hassled you puts you in a stronger negotiating position.

6 Don't mistake a friendly claim adjuster for a friend. Remember you're in a business negotiation.

7 Avoid venting anger and frustration on your insurer, but make sure they know you intend to hold them to their promises and duties.

8 Document that you're being cooperative. Even if you're frustrated, avoid saying or writing things that may make you seem uncooperative or the cause of delays or problems.

9 Be cautious. Don't sign a release, confidentiality or non-disclosure agreement without consulting with an attorney. An overly broad or premature release or non-disclosure agreement can weaken your position and ability to obtain full policy benefits.

10 The 4 "P"s: Be Polite, prompt, professional and persistent.

Additional claim guidance is available free of charge on our website at: www.uphelp.org.

"SPEAK UP"

Strong as possible

Paperwork organized

Empowered

Assertive but polite

Keeping a claim diary

Unwilling to be shortchanged

Pro-active

Appendix: Worksheets

(?) QUESTIONS TO ASK ...
When Buying a Home Policy

☐ How much per square foot will my home be insured for?

_____

_____

_____

☐ Will this policy be adequate if I have a total loss?

_____

_____

_____

Will it cover the cost of rebuilding my home to its pre-loss condition, including demolition, debris removal and replacement of the foundation, roof, electrical and plumbing to current codes?

_____

_____

_____

☐ What causes of loss are not covered?

_____

_____

_____

_____

☐ What items are subject to limits or exclusions and for which of these limits or exclusions should I consider adding coverage?

_____

_____

_____

☐ How much can I save if I increase my deductible? Is there more than one deductible in the policy? Is the deductible waived if there is a large loss?

_____

_____

_____

☐ Is my personal property covered for Replacement or Actual Cash Value? If replacement value is not included, what would it cost to add this coverage?

_____

_____

_____

☐ Will my insurance cover the cost to upgrade electrical, plumbing and other systems if I have to make repairs after a loss?

_____

_____

_____

☐ For how long will my temporary rent and related expenses be covered while my home is being repaired or rebuilt after a loss? Is there a total dollar cap, monthly cap or time limit on this coverage?

_____

_____

_____

☐ Is my Coverage E (Personal Liability) limit enough to protect my assets and future income? If not, what does umbrella coverage cost?

_____

_____

_____

☐ What discounts are available?

_____

_____

_____

☐ Will this policy cover all of the residents of my household even if they are not legally related or do I need to add their names to the policy?

_____

_____

_____

☐ If someone sues me, will my liability coverage pay for legal fees?

_____

_____

_____

☐ Do I have enough coverage to replace my unique or special items such as electronics, piano, jewelry, fine art, oriental rugs, wine, collectibles, etc.?

_____

_____

_____

☐ What are my options for insuring my home-based business property and operations?

_____

_____

_____

☐ If only a part of my roof or siding gets damaged, will this policy pay to replace all the shingles or siding so it matches?

_____

_____

_____

☐ Does the age of my roof matter?

_____

_____

_____

☐ Does this policy exclude or cap coverage for mold damage? What about water damage?

_____

_____

_____

☐ What are this insurance company's rules for premium increases and non-renewals if I file a claim?

_____

_____

_____

QUESTIONS TO ASK ...
When Buying A Renters Policy

☐ Will this policy cover the cost of repairing or replacing my
personal property and relocating me if the home or apartment
I am renting is damaged or destroyed in a fire, earthquake,
hurricane or flood?

_____

_____

_____

☐ What risks are not covered and should I add coverage for them?

_____

_____

_____

☐ For how long will my temporary rent and relocation expenses be
covered after a loss?

_____

_____

_____

☐ Is there a total dollar cap, monthly cap or time limit on temporary
rent coverage?

_____

_____

_____

☐ Do benefits stop once I've relocated?

_____

_____

_____

☐ What if my new rent is higher?

_____

_____

_____

☐ Will this policy allow me to replace my unique or special possessions such as electronics, musical instruments, jewelry, fine art, wine, collectibles, etc.?

_____

_____

_____

☐ Is my personal property coverage for Replacement or only Actual Cost Value? If replacement value is not included, what would be the cost to upgrade from Actual Cost Value?

_____

_____

_____

☐ Is my personal liability limit adequate to protect my assets? If not, what does umbrella coverage cost?

_____

_____

_____

☐ Will this policy cover all of the residents of my household even if they are not legally related or do I need to add their names to the policy?

_____

_____

_____

☐ How much can I save by increasing my deductible?

_____

_____

_____

☐ What are this insurance company's rules for premium increases and non-renewals if I file a claim?

_____

_____

_____

QUESTIONS TO ASK ...
When Buying An Auto Policy

☐ Is it worth buying Collision and/or Comprehensive coverage for my current car?

_____

_____

_____

☐ How much can I save by increasing my deductible?

_____

_____

_____

☐ Do I have enough Uninsured and Underinsured Motorist coverage?

_____

_____

_____

☐ Do I have coverage for a rental car while my car is in the shop for repairs?

_____

_____

_____

☐ I want liability limits that will protect my assets after a serious accident. Will this policy do that?

_____

_____

_____

☐ Will my policy pay for genuine OEM (Original Equipment Manufacturer) parts or only for cheaper "after-market" or "crash" parts?

_____

_____

_____

☐ Can I select the auto body repair shop of my choice?

_____

_____

_____

☐ Am I getting all the discounts I am eligible for?

_____

_____

_____

☐ For multiple drivers or cars in one household: am I better off insuring all the drivers on one policy, or should I opt for separate policies?

_____

_____

_____

☐ How will you (the insurance company) value my car if it's totaled?

_____

_____

_____

☐ What will happen if I think my car's a total loss but you (the insurance company) don't?

_____

_____

_____

☐ What will my insurance cover if I rent a car and get in an accident?

_____

_____

_____

☐ If I buy this policy, will I still need to pay for CDW and/or liability coverage when renting a car?

_____

_____

_____

☐ What are this insurance company's rules for post-claim rate increases and non-renewals?

_____

_____

_____

? **QUESTIONS TO ASK ...**
When Buying An Umbrella Policy

☐ Will this policy protect my and my household members' current assets and future earnings?

_____

_____

_____

☐ How much would it cost to increase the limits by an additional $1 or $2 million?

_____

_____

_____

☐ Will the policy cover all of my unique risk exposures (especially those not covered in my home and auto insurance or my employer's policies)?

_____

_____

_____

☐ Does my basic home/auto/renters policy have the minimum liability limits required by the terms of the umbrella policy?

_____

_____

_____

☐ Will the umbrella policy cover contractual indemnification liabilities that I assume when I sign contracts with rental agencies, caterers and other service providers?

_____

_____

_____

☐ Will the cost of legal defense be covered within the limit of my umbrella liability coverage or in addition to that limit? Are my combined limits adequate to cover both legal defense and settlement costs?

_____

_____

☐ Does the umbrella policy provide additional coverage for uninsured or underinsured motorists above what's covered by my car insurance policy?

_____

_____

_____

☐ Does this policy cover me when I'm driving a rental car?

_____

_____

_____

Index

B

bodily injury protection, 4, 52

body shop selection, 56–57

bracing for earthquakes, 33

brokers

  about, 9–11

  auto insurance, 58

  reasons to use, 8–9

building codes and replacement costs, 25

bundling, 11, 67

business travel, 61–62

C

cancellation, 4, 67

captive agents, 10

car insurance. *See* auto insurance

car rentals, 59–62

CDW (collision damage waivers), 59–62

charitable aid, 19

claims

  bundling and, 11

  communicating with insurance company about, 77–79

  decision about making, 74–75

  non-renewal after, 12

  notification of insurance company time limits, 74–75

  rate increases after, 12, 55, 74

  rental cars, 62

  risk category and making, 21, 55

  tips for, 76

CLUE (Comprehensive Loss and Underwriting Exchange), 4, 30

code upgrade coverage, 25

collision/comprehensive coverage

  defined, 4, 51

  need for, 53

  rental cars, 60

collision damage waivers (CDW), 59–62

combined single limits, 52

commercial pursuits exclusions

  home insurance, 31, 36

  rental cars, 59

  renters insurance, 46

  ride-sharing services, 50

commissions, 9

communication with insurance companies, 77–79

comparison shopping

  after non-renewal, 15

  auto insurance, 55

  bundling and, 11

sub-limits, 26–27, 31
loans after disasters, 27
loss of use, 51. *See also*
 additional living expenses
loyalty discounts, 54
LPI (lender placed) insurance, 13
Lyft, 50

M

Market Assistance programs, 15
marriage, 35, 45
medical expense coverage, 50,
 52, 54, 56
misrepresentation, rescission and,
 7

N

named perils policies, 25
National Flood Insurance
 Program (NFIP), 28
negotiation, claims as, 76, 78
non-admitted insurers, 13
non-disclosure agreements, 78
non-OEM parts, 56–57
non-owner auto policies, 50
non-renewal
 after claims, 12

defined, 6
shopping for new plan after, 15
notekeeping. *See* documentation/
 note-taking

O

original equipment manufacturer
 (OEM), 56–57
ownership transfers, 35, 58

P

parties at rental homes, 46
payments/premiums, 7. *See also*
 cost
peace of mind, 69
personal excess liability
 coverage, 7. *See also* exclusions
 and limitations; umbrella
 coverage
personal injury protection (PIP)
 amount to purchase, 54, 56
 defined, 52
 generally, 50
personal property
 changes in ownership of, 34, 45
 Coverage C for, 20
 inventory of, 32–33, 43–44

tailoring of coverage for, 26–27

pets, 36, 46

PIP (personal injury protection). *See* personal injury protection (PIP)

policies, defined, 6

policyholders, defined, 6

pool insurance, 13–14

pre-loss documentation of property, 32–33

premiums, defined, 7. *See also* cost

preparation, importance of, 3

price optimization, 54

pricing. *See* cost

professional appraisal method of insurance adequacy, 24

professional insurance salespeople, 9–11

professionalism, 77

pro rata refunds, 67

public/private hybrid insurance, 13–14

purchases of new homes, 35

R

rainy day funds, 14

rates, defined, 7. *See also* cost

ratings, 13

RC (replacement cost), 43

RCV (replacement cost value), 26

real estate value, 25

reconsideration, request for, 15

refunds, 67

releases, 78

remodeling, 34

renewal. *See* non-renewal

rental cars, 59–62

renters

  commercial pursuits exclusions, 31, 36, 46

  Section 8, 43

  umbrella coverage and, 68

renters insurance

  about, 42

  co-signing of leases, 46

  events triggering reconsideration of, 45–46

  questions to ask worksheet, 47–48, 89–91

  reasons to obtain, 42–43

  selection considerations for, 43–45

replacement cost (RC), 43

replacement cost estimates, 24

replacement cost value (RCV), 26

Made in the USA
San Bernardino, CA
01 December 2016